T0372603

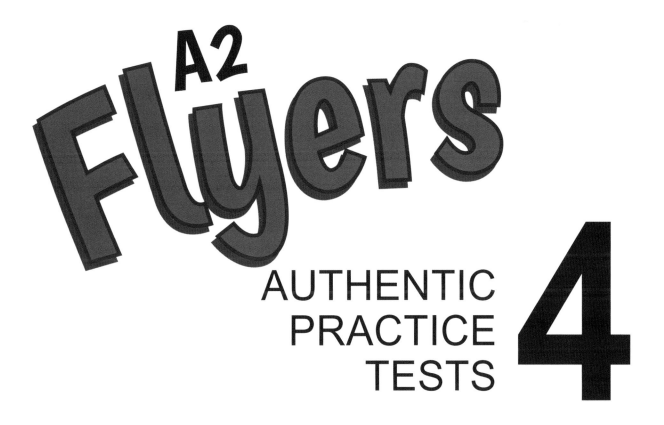

A2
Flyers

AUTHENTIC PRACTICE TESTS

4

STUDENT'S BOOK

WITH ANSWERS

WITH AUDIO

WITH RESOURCE BANK

Cambridge University Press

www.cambridge.org/elt

Cambridge Assessment English

www.cambridgeenglish.org

Information on this title: www.cambridge.org/9781009036283

© Cambridge University Press and Cambridge Assessment English 2022

This publication is in copyright. Subject to statutory exception
and to the provisions of relevant collective licensing agreements,
no reproduction of any part may take place without the written
permission of Cambridge University Press.

First published 2022

20 19 18 17 16 15 14 13 12 11 10

Printed in Poland by Opolgraf

A catalogue record for this publication is available from the British Library

ISBN 978-1-009-03628-3 Student's Book with Answers with Audio with Resource Bank
ISBN 978-1-009-03625-2 Student's Book without Answers with Audio

The publishers have no responsibility for the persistence or accuracy of URLs
for external or third-party internet websites referred to in this publication, and
do not guarantee that any content on such websites is, or will remain, accurate
or appropriate. Information regarding prices, travel timetables, and other factual
information given in this work is correct at the time of first printing but the
publishers do not guarantee the accuracy of such information thereafter.

The authors and publishers acknowledge the following sources of copyright material and are grateful
for the permissions granted. While every effort has been made, it has not always been possible to
identify the sources of all the material used, or to trace all copyright holders. If any omissions are
brought to our notice, we will be happy to include the appropriate acknowledgements on reprinting
and in the next update to the digital edition, as applicable.

Illustrations: Cambridge Assessment

Audio production by dsound recording studios

Typeset by QBS Learning

Cover illustration: Leo Trinidad/Astound

Contents

Part 1
– 5 questions –

Listening test audio

Listen and draw lines. There is one example.

Katy   Robert   Oliver   Helen

Sophia   Michael   Emma

Part 2
– 5 questions –

Listening test audio

Listen and write. There is one example.

Holly's homework

School subject		.... history ....
1	Name of teacher:	Mr ....
2	Read about person who invented:	the ....
3	Number of questions:	....
4	Must give homework to teacher on:	....
5	What to take to school:	some ....

Part 3
– 5 questions –

Listening test audio

William is helping his aunt to tidy her table.
Where did each thing on the table come from?

Listen and write a letter in each box. There is one example.

comb   H

letter

soap

scissors

bracelet

belt

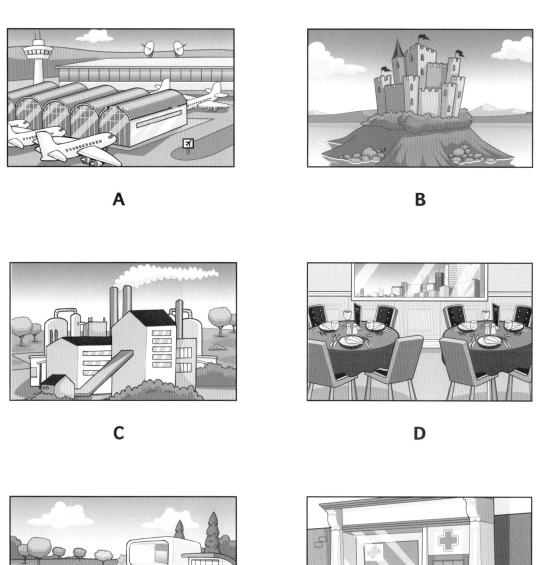

A

B

C

D

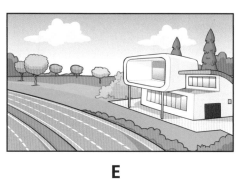

E

F

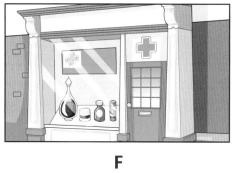

G

H

Part 4
– 5 questions –

Listening test audio

Listen and tick (✔) the box. There is one example.

Which sport is David going to play?

A ✔   B ☐   C ☐

1 Where will the match be?

A ☐   B ☐   C ☐

2 How will David get to the match?

A ☐   B ☐   C ☐

3   What time will the match begin?

A ☐   B ☐   C ☐

4   Who asked David to play in the match?

A ☐   B ☐   C ☐

5   How is David feeling now?

A ☐   B ☐   C ☐

Part 5
– 5 questions –

Listening test audio

Listen and colour and write. There is one example.

Part 1

– 10 questions –

Look and read. Choose the correct words and write them on the lines. There is one example.

a cave   a waiter   a meal   a cook

a mechanic

sugar

This place is dark and cold. Bats often live here.   ...... a cave ......

1 People use milk to make this white food. Many people like to eat it for breakfast with honey.   ....

2 This person can fly a rocket into space.   ....

3 Camels often live in this hot dry place, where there is only a little water.   ....

4 Farmers close this when they want to keep their animals inside the fields.   ....

5 This person is good at drawing and might have paintings in a museum.   ....

6 People usually use metal to make this. We hold it in our hand to eat our food.   ....

7 If you have problems with your car, you take it to this person.   ....

8 This person can work in a restaurant or a hotel. They bring food to people.   ....

9 If you want to go over a river you have to walk across this.   ....

10 This is sweet and people use it when they make chocolate and cakes.   ....

---

yoghurt

a planet

a bridge

an astronaut

an artist

a desert

air   a gate   a fork

Part 2
– 5 questions –

Michael is talking to Emma. What does Emma say?

Read the conversation and choose the best answer.
Write a letter (A–H) for each answer.

You do not need to use all the letters. There is one example.

Example

Michael: Did you do anything special for your birthday, Emma?

Emma: ....D...................

Questions

1 **Michael:** Cool! Pizza's my favourite food!

   Emma: ....

2 **Michael:** What do you like on top of your pizza?

   Emma: ....

3 **Michael:** I like different things on my pizza, like pineapple!

   Emma: ....

4 **Michael:** So, do you often have pizza?

   Emma: ....

5 **Michael:** Mum says we can make pizza tomorrow. Come to our house after school if you're not busy.

   Emma: ....

A   Nothing much. Usually just some tomato and olives.

B   No. Only once a month because my little brother hates it.

C   I'm sorry, I can't. We're having dinner at the moment.

D   My grandparents took me to my favourite pizza restaurant, actually. **(Example)**

E   Really? That's strange! I hate fruit on my pizza.

F   That would be brilliant, but I'll have to speak to my mum first.

G   It's mine, too. I prefer it to everything else.

H   Yes, we did. We found out about it yesterday.

Part 3
– 6 questions –

Read the story. Choose a word from the box. Write the correct word next to numbers 1–5. There is one example.

Example				
excited	surprise	late	bored	deepest
somewhere	worst	ago	explored	traffic

Holly was .... *excited* .... because she was going with her family

to visit her grandparents' house at the beach. 'Can we go swimming before

lunch?' asked Holly.

'Good idea!' said Dad. But there was a lot of **(1)** ....

on the motorway.

'Now we won't have time to go swimming,' said Holly.

After two hours, Holly said, 'I'm really hungry now. Can we stop to have

lunch **(2)** ....?'

'No, we're already very **(3)** .... for lunch at

Grandma's!' said Mum.

Holly said, 'This is the **(4)** .... journey ever!'

But when they were on Grandma and Grandpa's road, Dad drove past

their house. 'Why didn't you stop?!' asked Holly. 'I'm very hungry.'

'I'm going to the beach. I need a swim,' answered Dad.

'But there aren't any cafés there,' said Holly.

'There are now,' said Dad. 'Your Grandma's just opened a new café there! We

didn't tell you because we wanted it to be a **(5)** .... !'

'That's amazing!' said Holly. 'Grandma's the best cook in the world!'

(6) Now choose the best name for the story.

Tick one box.

Grandma's new house	☐
Holly's long journey	☐
Dad's fast car	☐

Part 4

– 10 questions –

Read the text. Choose the right words and write them on the lines.

Tortoises

Tortoises are animals that have four legs and a hard shell

Example ....on........................ their backs. There isn't only one kind of

1 tortoise and .... tortoise's shell is a different

shape. They have short legs and toes, and they do not have

2 .... teeth.

They pull their heads and necks inside their shells when they

3 .... afraid of something.

4 Tortoises eat plants, but there are some tortoises ....

5 eat snails and birds. Tortoises like to sleep for ....

of the day.

6 Some tortoises live .... they are very old.

7 A few live .... than 100 years! And on some

8 islands, there are very large tortoises. .... tortoises

9 have lots of food to eat, ... the animals grow big.

10 .... the weather gets cold, tortoises go to sleep

for months.

Example	on	up	out
1	each	another	both
2	every	any	no
3	feel	feels	felt
4	which	what	where
5	many	such	most
6	during	until	through
7	long	longer	longest
8	These	Them	This
9	because	so	or
10	Soon	When	Perhaps

Part 5
– 7 questions –

Look at the picture and read the story. Write some words to complete the sentences about the story. You can use 1, 2, 3 or 4 words.

The castle

Last weekend, Richard and his parents decided to visit a famous castle. They wanted to spend the day there, so Richard's dad prepared a picnic and Richard's mum put some umbrellas, a camera and all the other things they needed in their rucksacks. Then they went to the station to catch the train.

The castle was enormous. 'I think this castle's very popular,' said Richard. 'How do you know?' asked Mum. 'Well, there are so many cars here,' answered Richard.

Dad bought three tickets. A woman was waiting at the entrance to take them on a tour of the castle. 'There has been a castle here for more than six centuries,' the woman told them. They learned about the famous people who once lived in the castle and about the secret room there. Richard was really interested in that.

'Has anyone ever found the room?' asked Richard.

'Not yet,' laughed the woman.

After that, they went outside to sit on the grass and have their picnic. But then it started to rain. 'Oh no!' said Mum.

'It's OK, Mum. We can eat later. Let's go into the castle again and find the secret room. Come on – it'll be exciting!' said Richard.

'OK,' laughed Mum. 'We can eat our picnic in the secret room!'

Examples

Richard went to visit a castle with his parents last ....weekend........... .

Before they left, Richard's dad .....prepared a picnic..... for everyone to eat.

Questions

1   Richard and his parents carried all their things in their
....

2   The family travelled by .... to the castle.

3   When Richard saw lots of cars in the car park, he knew the castle was ....

4   They went .... of the castle and visited many of the old rooms.

5   A .... gave them some interesting information about the history of the castle.

6   While they were sitting on the .... outside, it began to rain.

7   Richard wanted to go into the castle again to look for the
....

Part 6

– 5 questions –

Read the diary page and write the missing words. Write one word on each line.

<u>**Saturday 10th March**</u>

Example Today I went to the shopping centre ....<u>with</u>..............
my parents. I wanted to use the money that Grandpa gave

1 .... to buy some new clothes for my school

2 trip. I needed a new .... of trainers and some
T-shirts. We went into lots of shops and I spent all the money

3 .... some expensive trainers.

4 In the evening, I took the dog for a .... in
the park.

5 .... that, we went home again and I watched
a film on TV.

Part 7

Look at the three pictures. Write about this story. Write **20** or more words.

....

....

....

....

....

....

Part 1

– 5 questions –

Listening test audio

Listen and draw lines. There is one example.

Harry   Betty   Michael   Sarah

Holly   Helen   George

Part 2
– 5 questions –

Listening test audio

Listen and write. There is one example.

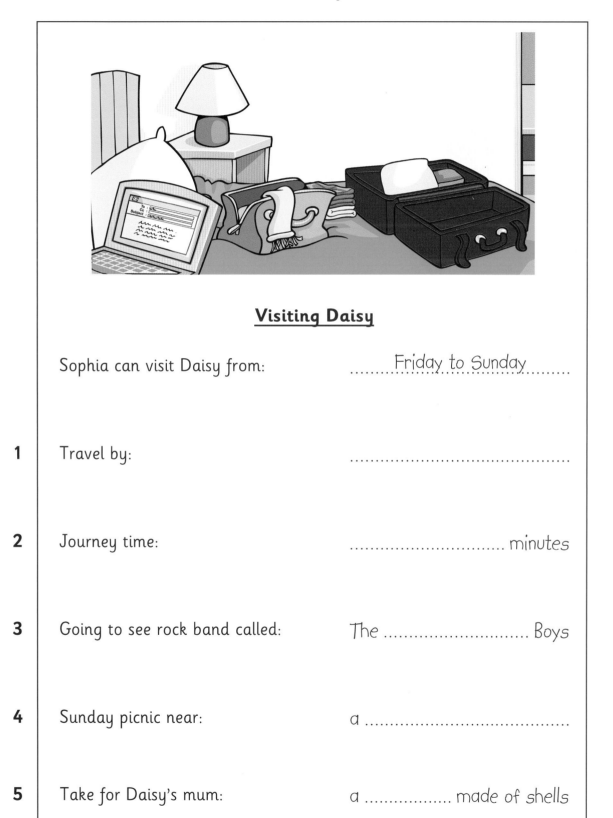

Visiting Daisy

Sophia can visit Daisy from:		Friday to Sunday
1	Travel by:	....
2	Journey time:	.... minutes
3	Going to see rock band called:	The .... Boys
4	Sunday picnic near:	a ....
5	Take for Daisy's mum:	a .... made of shells

Part 3

– 5 questions –

Listening test audio

Where did Lucy's class go with each teacher?

Listen and write a letter in each box. There is one example.

sports teacher   B

maths teacher   ☐

art teacher   ☐

science teacher   ☐

geography teacher   ☐

history teacher   ☐

A

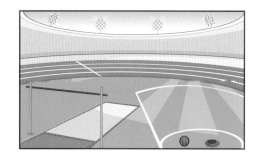

B

C

D

E

F

G

H

Part 4

– 5 questions –

Listening test audio

Listen and tick (✔) the box. There is one example.

What did Uncle Robert do with his friends last night?

A ✔   B ☐   C ☐

1 Where should Katy put the clean glasses?

A ☐   B ☐   C ☐

2 What did Uncle Robert and his friends eat?

A ☐   B ☐   C ☐

3   Who is the best player in the football team?

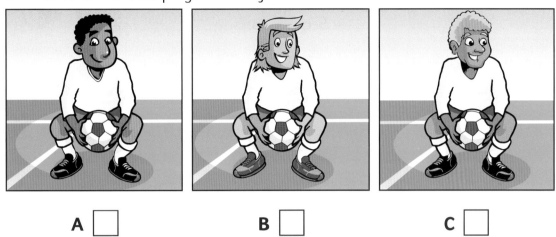

A ☐   B ☐   C ☐

4   Which sport is Uncle Robert best at?

A ☐   B ☐   C ☐

5   What does Uncle Robert want to show Katy later?

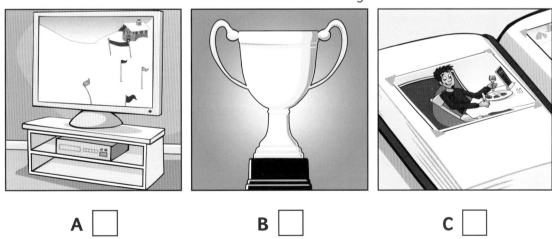

A ☐   B ☐   C ☐

Part 5

– 5 questions –

Listening test audio

Listen and colour and write. There is one example.

Part 1
– 10 questions –

Look and read. Choose the correct words and write them on the lines. There is one example.

factories   glue   a uniform   a subject

a shelf   a stadium

castles   a timetable

a hotel   a belt

a chemist   a necklace

	In stories, kings and queens usually live in these old buildings.	*castles*
1	If you want to cut some paper you can use these.	....
2	You use this to repair things when they are broken.	....
3	You can wear this around your trousers if they are too big.	....
4	These are usually large. People work in them and make things like cars.	....
5	Students look at this to find out when their lessons start and end.	....
6	Police officers and nurses have to put this on before they start work.	....
7	Actors work on a stage in this place.	....
8	You can use this to help you understand and spell words.	....
9	People go here to watch football matches or sometimes to see a pop concert.	....
10	When you are on holiday you might stay in one of these.	....

a theatre   scissors   a dictionary

Part 2
– 5 questions –

Helen is talking to her new friend Michael. Helen is asking Michael about his hobby, cooking. What does Michael say?

Read the conversation and choose the best answer.
Write a letter (A–H) for each answer.

You do not need to use all the letters. There is one example.

Example

Helen: Who taught you to cook, Michael?

Michael: ....B...........................

Questions

1 Helen: Why do you like cooking?

Michael: ....

2 Helen: Where do you get ideas about new things to cook?

Michael: ....

3 Helen: Do your parents help you cook?

Michael: ....

4 Helen: What's your favourite thing to cook?

Michael: ....

5 Helen: Can you teach me to make a cake?

Michael: ....

A	From the videos that I watch online.
B	My grandma did. She makes great cakes. **(Example)**
C	Of course. Why don't you come to my house tomorrow?
D	It's fun, and I enjoy eating all the things I make.
E	Perhaps. I burnt them all!
F	Biscuits. They're easy to make and they always taste good.
G	Yes. It tasted like pizza.
H	Sometimes, but I do a lot by myself.

Part 3
– 6 questions –

Read the story. Choose a word from the box. Write the correct word next to numbers 1–5. There is one example.

Example				
built	furry	keeping	hurried	interested
entrance	collect	torch	missing	sound

Harry and his family went to the beach last week. In the morning, Harry and his sister Katy ....*built*................. sand castles. After lunch, Mum said, 'There are some caves on this beach. Would you like to explore them?' 'Yes,' said Harry, but Katy decided to stay with her father. 'We're going to **(1)** .... some shells,' she said.

After a short walk, Mum and Harry found the **(2)** .... to the caves. They climbed over the rocks and went inside. 'I can't see anything because it's so dark,' said Harry. 'Don't worry,' said Mum. 'I've got a **(3)** ....' She turned it on. Suddenly Harry shouted 'What are all those **(4)** .... creatures flying around?' Mum started laughing. 'They're bats!' she said. 'They won't hurt you. They're amazing!'

They **(5)** .... back to Dad and Katy. 'We saw a hundred bats!' shouted Harry. 'Well, we've got two hundred wonderful shells!' said Katy.

(6) Now choose the best name for the story.

Tick one box.

Harry and Mum get lost ☐

Lunch in a cave ☐

Bats and shells at the beach ☐

Part 4

– 10 questions –

Read the text. Choose the right words and write them on the lines.

Swans

Example	A swan is a bird ....which.......... always lives near water.
1	It is like a duck, but much .... , with a very
	long neck. Swans have heavy bodies, but their wings are very strong
2	.... they can fly well.
	Swans can sleep in or out of the water, and they can
3	.... go to sleep when they are standing on one leg!
	Swans live in several different countries. They are
4	.... white, but in some places there are black ones
5	too. Most swans fly to warmer countries .... the
	winter starts. This is called 'migration'.
	A baby swan is called a 'cygnet'. Cygnets are grey and can swim as
6	.... as they come out of their eggs. A mother swan
7	often carries her young cygnets .... her back when
8	she's swimming. She does this to keep .... safe.
	Swans are clever birds. If a person does something unkind to a swan, it
9	will .... that person. You shouldn't go too near to
10	a swan – they can sometimes .... dangerous.

Example	which	it	where
1	large	larger	largest
2	so	while	after
3	ever	instead	also
4	later	usually	yet
5	before	during	since
6	far	soon	much
7	on	in	by
8	it	us	them
9	remembered	remember	remembers
10	being	be	been

Part 5
– 7 questions –

Look at the picture and read the story. Write some words to complete the sentences about the story. You can use 1, 2, 3 or 4 words.

Emma wins a competition

Emma was bored. It was Saturday afternoon and all her friends were busy. Then her mum showed her the newspaper. 'Look!' she said. There was some information about an art competition. The post office wanted children to design a new stamp. 'It says you should send them your best picture of an insect,' said Mum.

Emma decided to enter the competition. 'I'll do a picture of a butterfly,' she said. She used lots of different colours and some special silver paint in her picture. She felt pleased with it. When she finished, Mum gave her a huge brown envelope. Emma put the picture inside. 'I'll send it tomorrow,' said Mum.

During the next week, Emma had lots of things to do, and she forgot about the competition. Then one day, when she came home from school, Mum said, 'There's a letter for you.' Emma didn't often get letters. She sat down, opened the envelope and read the letter. Then she jumped up and shouted 'I've won the competition!' She was very excited.

A few days later, a journalist came to Emma's house. She asked Emma some questions about her picture. There was a photographer with the journalist. He took some photos of Emma and her design.

Emma's prize for winning the competition was some beautiful pencils, and she thinks it is amazing to see her stamp on everyone's letters.

Examples

Emma was feeling bored because ..her friends were busy.. .

Emma's mum found some information in a ....newspaper............
about a competition.

Questions

1   To enter the competition, children needed to design a stamp with an

.... on it.

2   Emma decided to draw a .... for her design.

3   Emma liked the colours and the .... in
her picture.

4   Emma .... because she had a very busy
week with lots to do.

5   When she read the letter about winning the competition,
Emma felt ....

6   A journalist and a .... visited Emma at
her house.

7   Emma won .... in the competition, and
loves seeing her stamp on letters.

Part 6

– 5 questions –

Read the diary entry and write the missing words. Write one word on each line.

Example	Today I played football for my school team. I .... *have* .... played for the team since the school year started. There
1	.... five of us in the football team. The match
2	was at another school and we went there ....
3	bus. I felt .... bit worried, but the other players on the team helped me feel better. We played really well.
4	I .... over in the middle of the match, but it
5	didn't hurt. Then I scored a .... , and my friend Sarah scored two more. It was a great match.

Part 7

Look at the three pictures. Write about this story. Write 20 or more words.

....

....

....

....

....

Part 1

– 5 questions –

Listening test audio

Listen and draw lines. There is one example.

Emma   Frank   Helen   George

Sophia   Harry   Katy

Part 2

– 5 questions –

Listening test audio

Listen and write. There is one example.

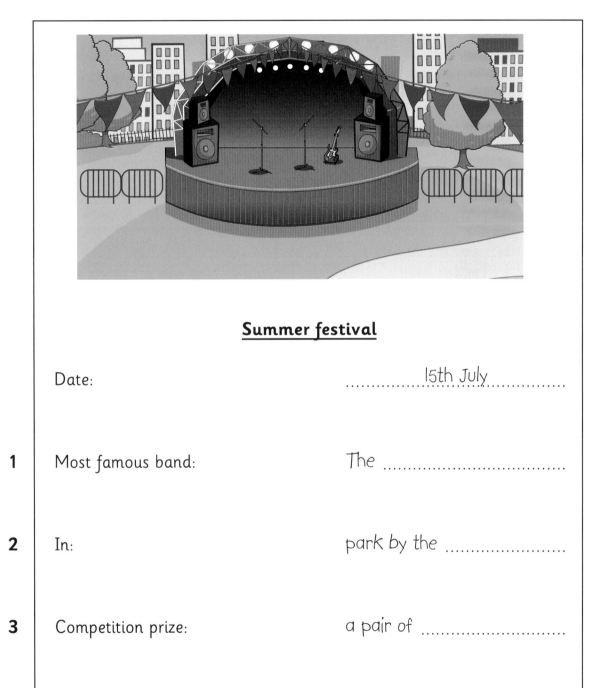

Summer festival

	Date:	15th July
1	Most famous band:	The ....
2	In:	park by the ....
3	Competition prize:	a pair of ....
4	Phone number for more information:	....
5	Take:	an ....

Part 3

– 5 questions –

Listening test audio

Holly's father is telling Holly about some things he found at home. What did he find in each place?

Listen and write a letter in each box. There is one example.

	balcony	A
	steps	☐
	cooker	☐
	gate	☐
	basement	☐
	swing	☐

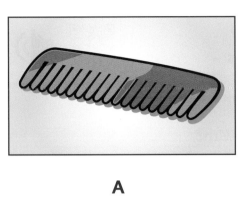

A

B

C

D

E

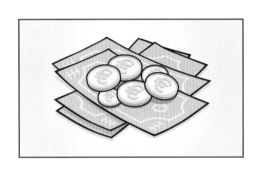

F

G

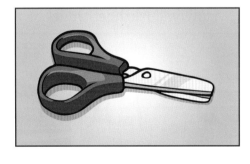

H

Part 4
– 5 questions –

Listening test audio

Listen and tick (✔) the box. There is one example.

Who is Michael going to go to the theatre with?

A ☐   B ☐   C ✔

1   How did Michael find out about the special evening at the theatre?

A ☐   B ☐   C ☐

2   How will Michael travel to the theatre?

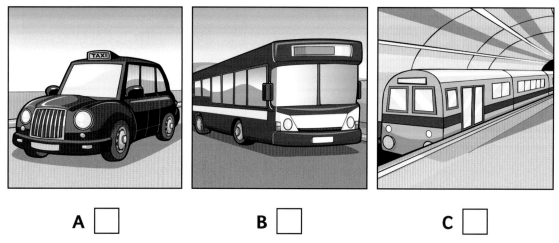

A ☐   B ☐   C ☐

3 What time does Michael want to arrive at the theatre?

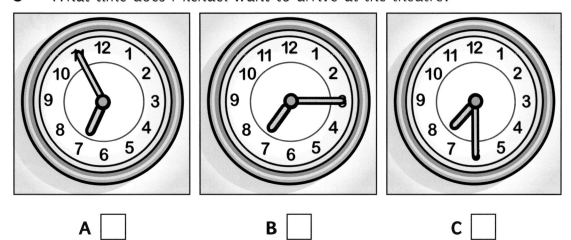

A ☐   B ☐   C ☐

4 What will Michael be most interested in?

A ☐   B ☐   C ☐

5 Where are the theatre tickets?

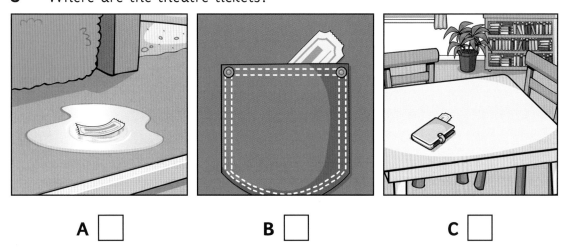

A ☐   B ☐   C ☐

Part 5
– 5 questions –

Listening test audio

Listen and colour and write. There is one example.

Part 1
– 10 questions –

Look and read. Choose the correct words and write them on the lines. There is one example.

a restaurant   gloves   an airport   olives

jam

trainers

strawberries

pyjamas

	You put these on when it is sunny outside, so you can see better.	sunglasses
1	This is a very tall building which often has apartments or offices in it.	....
2	Some people sleep in these clothes in bed at night to keep warm.	....
3	These are often made of wool. People wear them on their hands when it's cold.	....
4	You go to this place when you want to catch a plane and fly somewhere.	....
5	People sometimes eat this with milk or yoghurt. You eat it in a bowl.	....
6	You should wear these on your feet when you go running or go to the gym.	....
7	This is where important people like kings and queens live. It is often very old.	....
8	People put these on pizzas. They're small and round and can be green or black.	....
9	These are a kind of fruit. They are red and they taste sweet.	....
10	This is where you go to have a nice meal. A waiter brings your food.	....

a uniform

a skyscraper

cookies

a castle

a police station   sunglasses   cereal

Part 2

– 5 questions –

Robert is talking to his friend, Holly. What does Holly say?

Read the conversation and choose the best answer.
Write a letter (A–H) for each answer.

You do not need to use all the letters. There is one example.

Example

Robert: What's your new school like?

Holly: .... D ....

Questions

1 **Robert:** What time do you start school every day?

Holly: ....

2 **Robert:** Which teacher do you like best?

Holly: ....

3 **Robert:** What's your favourite subject?

Holly: ....

4 **Robert:** Do you cycle to school?

Holly: ....

5 **Robert:** Have you got lots of new friends?

Holly: ....

A   Mr Black, because he's kind and we have a lot of fun in his classes.

B   I've got a few! We have lunch together and chat when we have a break.

C   At quarter past eight, and we finish at half past three.

D   It's amazing! Everyone's very friendly and the lessons are really interesting. **(Example)**

E   I'd like to, but it's too far and there's a lot of traffic.

F   Of course I can, but only after school.

G   I like them all, but I think geography's the most interesting.

H   Sometimes I feel bored in Mrs Sugar's science lessons.

Part 3
– 6 questions –

Read the story. Choose a word from the box. Write the correct word next to numbers 1–5. There is one example.

Example				
ended	space	lovely	hope	summer
late	concert	explain	middle	wish

Emma was watching a TV programme for children. It was about festivals in different countries. Before the programme ....*ended*............ the man on TV said, 'OK, now I'm going to **(1)** .... how you can enter today's competition! We'd like you to draw a picture of a festival that you've been to and send your picture to me.'

Emma sat and thought about the programme. 'I know! I'll draw a picture of the music festival in our town last **(2)** .... ,' she decided. She borrowed her brother's pencils and found some paper.

'That's a **(3)** .... picture! I like it very much,' her mother said. 'I'm sure you'll win the competition!'

'I really **(4)** .... so,' said Emma, and she went to post her picture to the man on TV.

A week later, Emma's mum shouted, 'Emma! Come downstairs. There's a letter for you!' Emma hurried downstairs and opened the envelope. 'I've won the competition, Mum!' she said. 'The prize is two tickets for a big

(5) .... next month in London!'

(6) Now choose the best name for the story.

Tick one box.

Emma gets some good news ☐

Emma's mum wins a competition ☐

Emma plays music at a festival ☐

Part 4
– 10 questions –

Read the text. Choose the right words and write them on the lines.

The history of golf

Example	Golf is a very popular game in ....many............... countries.
1	The place where people play golf .... called a
	'golf course'. There are about 32,000 golf courses in the world and
2	the .... one is 400 years old. This is in Scotland,
3	.... has some of the best golf courses in the world.
4	The kind of golf that people play today .... in
5	Scotland more than five hundred years ....
	Most big golf courses have 18 holes. Players try to hit a small ball into
6	.... hole on the golf course by only hitting the ball
	a few times.
7	.... there were golf courses, people played
8	.... beaches and hit stones into holes in the sand.
9	Golf courses .... to have lots of space and very
	green grass. In some countries where it doesn't rain a lot, this can
10	.... a problem because they need to use a lot of
	water to keep the grass green.

Example	many	much	both
1	has	does	is
2	old	older	oldest
3	who	which	when
4	start	starts	started
5	already	ago	ever
6	each	another	such
7	If	So	Before
8	on	under	for
9	need	could	must
10	been	being	be

Part 5

– 7 questions –

Look at the picture and read the story. Write some words to complete the sentences about the story. You can use 1, 2, 3 or 4 words.

The lost racing car

George was unhappy because he couldn't find his new toy racing car. It was a silver car and George loved playing with it. But now it was missing.

'Perhaps I lost it while I was playing in my bedroom,' he thought, and went to look for it there. He couldn't see the car anywhere, so he went into the living room and looked under all the cushions on the sofa. Then he looked behind the sofa, but it wasn't there. Then he rang his friend, William. He sometimes played at William's house. 'Is my racing car there?' he asked. 'No, it isn't. Sorry, George,' said William. 'What am I going to do?' George thought.

'Have you seen my car?' he asked his mum. 'No,' she said. 'Go outside and look in the garden.' He found a tennis ball in the grass, but his car wasn't there. Then he went to look in the big tree in the middle of the garden. He could see a large nest in the tree. Suddenly, a beautiful black and white bird flew into the nest. It was carrying something silver. 'Perhaps the bird has taken my silver car!' George thought. After the bird flew away again, George climbed the tree and looked inside the nest. His car was there. 'Wow! That's lucky,' George thought. 'What a strange place to find it!'

Examples

George was sad because his new racing car was ....missing.............. .

First, George looked for his car ....in his bedroom........ but it wasn't there.

Questions

1 In the living room, George looked .... and behind the sofa for his car.

2 George decided to phone .... , but the racing car wasn't at his house.

3 George's mum wanted him to look ....

4 There was a .... in the grass, but not his car.

5 George saw that there was a big .... in the tree.

6 The black and white bird had .... in its mouth.

7 When the bird .... , George found his car in the bird's nest.

Part 6
– 5 questions –

Read the diary entry and write the missing words. Write one word on each line.

Example	I .... *went* .... to the museum today with my friend,
1	Sarah. We learned .... extinct animals. First,
	a man gave us a tour of the museum and then we went to explore.
	On the top floor we found a model of a huge animal. It looked
2	.... an elephant but it had much more hair.
3	This animal lived a long time ago and it ....
	called a 'mammoth'. When Sarah touched the model, it moved and
4	it .... a frightening noise! We were really
5	surprised and then we laughed .... lot.

Part 7

Look at the three pictures. Write about this story. Write **20** or more words.

....

....

....

....

....

....

Blank Page

Blank Page

Candidate's copy

Find the Differences

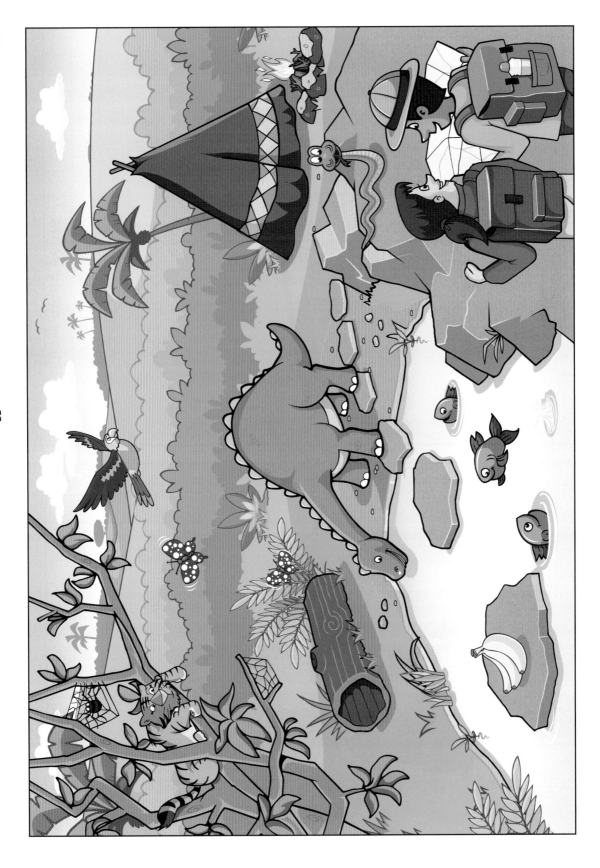

Information Exchange

Helen's new book

name	The Circus Clown
where / buy	supermarket
when / buy	Saturday
how many pages	200
funny / sad	funny

Harry's new book

name	?
where / buy	?
when / buy	?
how many pages	?
funny / sad	?

Candidate's copy

Information Exchange

Helen's new book

name	?
where / buy	?
when / buy	?
how many pages	?
funny / sad	?

Harry's new book

name	The Snowman
where / buy	bookshop
when / buy	yesterday
how many pages	145
funny / sad	sad

Examiner's and Candidate's copy

Picture Story

Mum and the fruit salad

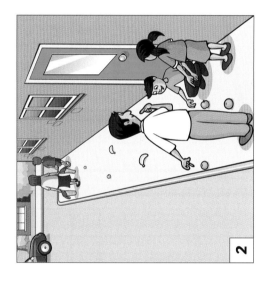

Ben   Mum

Blank Page

Examiner's copy

Find the Differences

Candidate's copy

Find the Differences

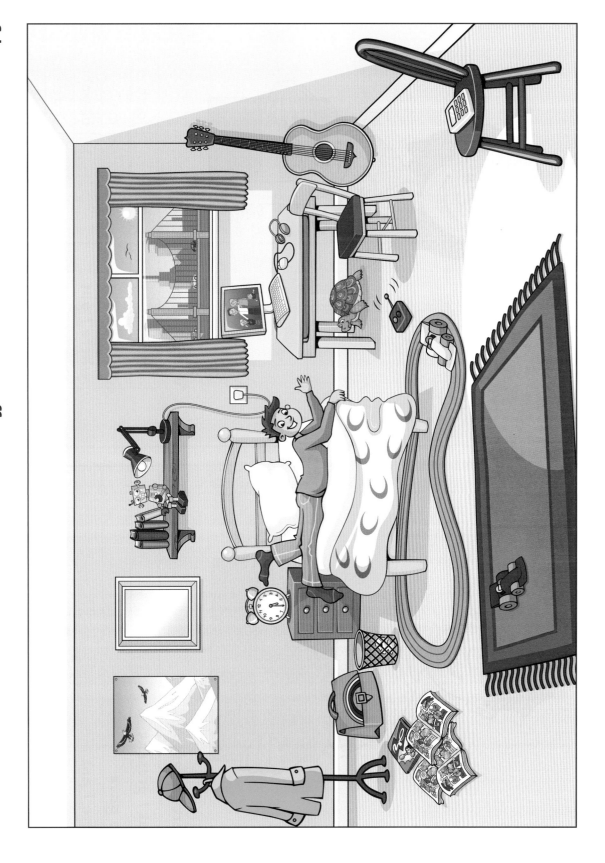

Information Exchange

Vicky's present

what / present	football shirt
who gave	aunt
where / put	bedroom
when / get	yesterday
colour	red and black

Robert's present

what / present	?
who gave	?
where / put	?
when / get	?
colour	?

Information Exchange

Vicky's present

what / present	?
who gave	?
where / put	?
when / get	?
colour	?

Robert's present

what / present	computer
who gave	uncle
where / put	living room
when / get	this morning
colour	grey

Picture Story

Examiner's and Candidate's copy

Peter and Charlie get lost

Peter   Charlie

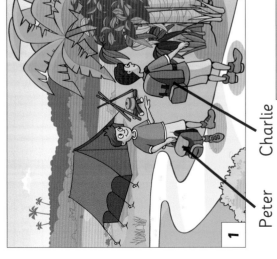

Blank Page

Examiner's copy

Find the Differences

Find the Differences

Information Exchange

Emma's sports club

where	Lake Road
day / go	Saturday
what sport / do	sailing
time / go	2.30
who / go with	best friend

Michael's sports club

where	?
day / go	?
what sport / do	?
time / go	?
who / go with	?

Candidate's copy

Information Exchange

Michael's sports club

where	Hill Street
day / go	Monday
what sport / do	tennis
time / go	6.30
who / go with	brother

Emma's sports club

where	?
day / go	?
what sport / do	?
time / go	?
who / go with	?

Picture Story   **Examiner's and Candidate's copy**

Tom and Betty go to the hospital

Tom   Betty

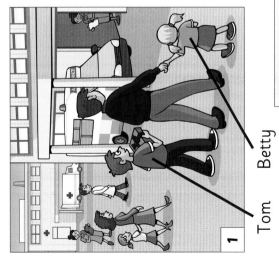

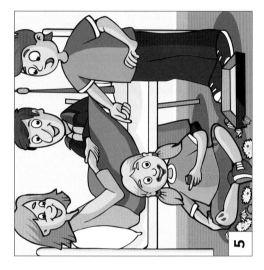

Blank Page

Blank Page

Blank Page

Blank Page